BOA ME NA ME BOA WO
"help me to help you"

Symbol of interdependence,
helpfulness and cooperation.

the wisdom chronicles

WHAT I WANT YOU TO KNOW

Natalie Lamb

Editorial Services: Marsha D. Phillips
Cover design and typesetting: Arjan van Woensel & Marisa Garau
Logo design: Zoe Lamb

ISBN # paperback: 978-1-961077-02-7
ISBN # ebook: 978-1-961077-03-4

Dedication

This book is dedicated to the children I birthed, Zoe and Talia,
and to the children I was blessed to help nurture,
Adam, Sophia and Liya.

When you arrived, I vowed to live a life you would be proud of.
You taught me the beauty of care and sacrifice. You added greater
worth to my life. I hope I have made you proud!

I am immensely grateful God allowed me to be an instrument in
your lives. I hope the music we made together is forever cherished
and the harmonies last your lifetimes.

We have an eternal love.
My heart beats with you all.
You have my love and devotion, always.

The Logo

When the logo for *It's Your Choice* was created, the West African symbols for four integral themes in life: Wisdom, Ingenuity, Patience, and Change were integrated to highlight these essential foundations for personal transformation.

Going clockwise, the first is **Wisdom** — the knowing and understanding that must be sought above all else, as being wise brings forth insights on why, how, and when to move — and when to be still.

Next, we have **Ingenuity**, the ability to be clever, unique, and inventive — skills needed to make your life tailor-fit.

Then we have **Patience** — a powerful virtue that is unfortunately often overlooked; to truly progress, it takes time to assess; it takes time to make changes.

Finally, we have **Change**, the great Constant. Life is ever evolving and knowledge and skills are needed to manage the natural ebbs and flows of life. All four —Wisdom, Ingenuity, Patience, and Change — are what *It's Your Choice* brings into focus.

what I want you to know

How to Use This Book to Guide Your Life

I wrote these words over many years. I pray they comfort you, teach you, assure you, and help you grow.

When you feel lost, may these words help you find home again. All of them will not fit where you are right now. When you need them, come back and explore these pages.

The lined areas are here for you to keep notes. Add to these words of wisdom as you grow and learn.

The blank pages at the back are here for you to grow and learn, and record your thoughts and realizations for the generations to come.

Let's write a book of wisdom together.

WHAT I WANT YOU TO KNOW

NATALIE LAMB

find the middle

∾ Live a balanced life. Don't swing too far left or right. Make a habit of finding the middle.

. . . .

. . . .

. . . .

. . . .

. . . .

. . . .

. . . .

. . . .

. . . .

. . . .

stay open

∼ Stay open. Always give yourself room to change ideas, beliefs, feelings, and passions. In this technological age, you can have extensive knowledge about many things. Gain as much knowledge as you can. Find joy in it. Ignorance is not bliss nor is it acceptable. Be willing to try different ways of doing things. Also remember, if something does not work for you, this does not mean it will not work for others. There is no need to put others down because you don't do it their way.

....

....

....

....

....

....

....

tell the truth

∽ Tell the truth. Dishonesty in any form is toxic for you and those around you.

....

....

....

....

....

....

....

....

....

....

....

what do you want?

~ Learn to articulate your wants more than your dislikes.

. . . .

. . . .

. . . .

. . . .

. . . .

. . . .

. . . .

. . . .

. . . .

. . . .

be clear

∿ Let others know how you feel. Be clear. The clearer you are, the less likely others can say they didn't understand and make excuses for their actions.

....

....

....

....

....

....

....

....

....

....

respect yourself

~ Give yourself the respect you want others to give you. If you're degrading yourself, others will too.

....

....

....

....

....

....

....

....

....

....

....

success has many forms

∼ There are many forms of success. You don't have to fit the mold to be successful. *You* define your success. Work from your heart and passion, not a society-imposed script.

. . . .

. . . .

. . . .

. . . .

. . . .

. . . .

. . . .

. . . .

. . . .

. . . .

simply be you

～ Find your group instead of trying to fit into one. It will change your life. It will give you more confidence to be yourself, a surety far too many don't have.

....

....

....

....

....

....

....

....

....

....

respect 'no'

∼ Stay away from people who will not respect and accept your nos. It is a sign of manipulation. It means they may harm you because what they want matters more than what you have expressed. Make sure you always respect others' nos as well.

....

....

....

....

....

....

....

....

....

stay calm

～ Stay calm. No one can rattle you unless you let them. A quiet pause gives you time to center yourself and move forward with little or no regrets.

....

....

....

....

....

....

....

....

....

....

it's the human condition

∼ Never carry shame. Shame often comes from our need to be perfect, invincible, and infallible. Once you can accept your human frailty, shame becomes a non-issue. We are all limited; it's the human condition. Our limitations are just reminders that we need God.

....

....

....

....

....

....

....

....

....

know what you can't tolerate

～ In your relationships, always tell people what you want and need, then leave it to them to decide if they will honor it. If they don't honor it to the best of their ability, you must then decide if you can tolerate the absence of your desire. If you can't tolerate that, move on—not with anger, but with the resolution that you deserve to have what you desire.

....

....

....

....

....

....

....

....

pray for wisdom

⌒ Pray for wisdom above all else. God said He gives wisdom freely if we ask. In every situation you face, good or bad, ask for wisdom, even more than blessings and relief. Wisdom is the key to life. Wisdom makes you rich in every area of your life. Seek knowledge then add your wisdom and you will be a force to reckon with.

....

....

....

....

....

....

....

....

choose well

～ Our life is simply the choices we make. Easy choices sometimes feel good in the moment but you may pay a high price in the end. We are constantly choosing. Choose well.

....

....

....

....

....

....

....

....

....

....

go after it

∼ Don't let the fear of what others may say dictate your life. If you want something, like something, want to try something, then go after it. People will always have an opinion. We all have a right to our opinions, but don't live a life based on the possible disapproval of others.

....

....

....

....

....

....

....

....

....

know your power

∼ There will always be difficult people to deal
with. You determine to what degree they bring
you discomfort. You determine how much
power they hold in your life, your day, and your
hour. Some people just need to be ignored.
Ignoring difficult people is a powerful skill.
It allows you to keep your power and it allows
them to see they are powerless in your life.

....

....

....

....

....

....

....

....

one day at a time

~ Embrace the simple things in life. Don't get distracted by money, fame, and glamour. Instead, relish what you need just for today. God's mercy and grace are renewed every morning so you only have to make it through each day.

....

....

....

....

....

....

....

....

....

work for it

∿ You are not entitled to anything—not love, money, opportunities, friendships, respect, etc. You must put in work for what you want. You want love? You must work to keep it. You want money? You must work for it. You want opportunities? You must embrace what is in front of you and be prepared for the opportunities that come. Never think you are owed anything.

....

....

....

....

....

....

....

....

change, don't complain

∼ Never sit back and just complain.
Either begin to create change or be quiet.
Complaining without acting has never created
change. Surround yourself with people who
are willing to build and watch out for folks who
didn't contribute but jump aboard after you
have put in the work.

....

....

....

....

....

....

....

....

....

practice self-awareness

∼ Practice self-awareness. Realize your
presence is part of the atmosphere. What
you do and say affects others and their
experiences. Every thought, opinion, belief
or concern does not always need to be shared.
Some things must remain mental notes for you
to learn from.

....

....

....

....

....

....

....

....

....

one-time event in history

〜 The world loves labels and putting you in a box. The only labels you need are "child of God" and your name. Never force yourself to conform for others' comfort or even your own. You are a one-time event in history. Write a fierce story for others to read when you're gone. Write a story that will make you proud!

. . . .

. . . .

. . . .

. . . .

. . . .

. . . .

. . . .

. . . .

. . . .

love your body

∼ Love your body. It's the only one you get. It may not be the size and shape you want but cherish it. Take care of it but don't get caught up in trying to make it like others'. Find the beauty in what you are and what you have today. If you want to work on your body, do it from a place of love, not disgust. Don't wait until it's "perfect." You don't have to like every crevice but respect and appreciate the body God gave you. Find peace in your imperfections. Exercise because it's good for your body, not out of obsession. Eat a good healthy balanced diet and never let food control you. Change what you can, not out of hate, but from the place of *I think change will be better for me*.

....

....

....

....

express gratitude

∽ As long as you are living and breathing, seek and express gratitude. Aging is going to happen if you keep living. Your body will betray you one day. Even if your body betrays you, find joys that will keep you going.

....

....

....

....

....

....

....

....

....

....

embrace the gift of NOW

∼ Learn to accept yourself as-is. Waiting for a change before embracing the gift of NOW is no way to live. Often, when you reach a goal, you may still be unhappy or discontent. It is always an inside job to live in happiness and contentment.

....

....

....

....

....

....

....

....

....

negativity can make you sick

∼ You may not have all you want and desire but train your mind to find things to smile about, laugh about, and rejoice in. Negativity can make you sick, even kill you.

....

....

....

....

....

....

....

....

....

....

what will be, will be

∼ What will be, will be. You never know what's around the corner and there is no sense in panicking over what might be. If it's meant to be, it will be. If it's not, find a way to accept this and move forward without the baggage of what could've been.

....

....

....

....

....

....

....

....

....

don't be in your winter gear
when summer has come

∼ Every season is not sunny. As much as you accept joy, you must accept sorrow. Study and truly digest Ecclesiastes 3—*There is a season for all things*. Know what season you are in and be aware that seasons change. Don't be in your winter gear when summer has come. Life is constantly moving, shifting. Know when to change your clothes.

. . . .

. . . .

. . . .

. . . .

. . . .

. . . .

. . . .

. . . .

rejection is a part of life

∼ Rejection is a part of life. It doesn't need to be taken personally all the time. A lot of times people reject you, your ideas, and your talents based on who and where they are in their life. Rejection hurts, but don't let it stop you. Sometimes a no is a gift wrapped up in some nasty paper. You may find it is a treasure as life unfolds.

....

....

....

....

....

....

....

....

....

death is a part of life

∼ Death changes your world. We will all die
many deaths. Many dreams and hopes will
die. Mourn, grieve, accept them, then create a
new normal in place of that death. That goes
for people too. The hole left from a loved one
stays. Create a new normal with the hole. Allow
yourself to find the beauty in life again, but
that can only be done if you properly grieve
and mourn.

....

....

....

....

....

....

....

....

don't stop too long

∽ The end of the road doesn't equal the end of a journey. As long as you are living you get to journey. Sometimes you need to sit back and take some serious deep breaths—calm down until newness finds you again. But don't stop too long. Playing catch-up is hard.

. . . .

. . . .

. . . .

. . . .

. . . .

. . . .

. . . .

. . . .

. . . .

embrace your weaknesses

∼ Our weaknesses are ways for God to show His perfect power. Trust me, you want to see that power often, so embrace your weaknesses and watch God show you things you never could obtain in your own strength.

....

....

....

....

....

....

....

....

....

....

pause and think

∽ Think before you act. Ask yourself, how will I feel about this in a day, week, or year? Know the difference between feeling good in the moment and feeling good in the long term. Don't get the two mixed up.

....

....

....

....

....

....

....

....

....

....

you get to change your mind

∼ Be a slave to nothing and no one. God doesn't even ask that of us. Let no one or nothing drag you around. Let no one or nothing make you believe you don't have a choice. Choice is a gift you can always give yourself. You get to change your mind if your last choice is no longer serving you well.

....

....

....

....

....

....

....

....

....

your choices make up your life

～ Put long decisive thought into your choices. Your choices make up your life, so see each choice as a possible game changer. Be logical and careful. Try not to make decisions in haste. Even when pressure is on you, find your quiet place to think and reflect. If anyone tries to take that from you, move away from them; they don't mean you any good.

....

....

....

....

....

....

....

....

don't live selfishly

∽ Don't live life selfishly. Life sometimes
requires you to sacrifice for others. Give to
those who need you. Show up when others
are too weak to stand. Giving will make you a
better person, but don't get that confused with
being a doormat. Your heart will guide you as
to when, where and who to give to. Trust it!

. . . .

. . . .

. . . .

. . . .

. . . .

. . . .

. . . .

. . . .

. . . .

never risk your integrity

∽ Fear no man so much that you risk your integrity and character. Take whatever consequences your choices give you but stand firm on honesty and truth.

. . . .

. . . .

. . . .

. . . .

. . . .

. . . .

. . . .

. . . .

. . . .

. . . .

*you are always
representing yourself*

∽ When you walk out the door, you are always representing yourself. No, you don't always need to be dressed up. Have some good-looking comfy clothes at easy access if you need to run out. There is no excuse for smelling bad and not combing your hair (if you are that rushed at least put on a hat). One way to make this a rule is to look good at home just for yourself, not every day but most days, even if you are just staying at home.

....

....

....

....

....

....

....

practice self-control

∼ Learn how to deny yourself sometimes. It's a great lesson in self-control.

....

....

....

....

....

....

....

....

....

....

use money wisely

∿ Use your money wisely. Money is a fickle friend. Sometimes it stands tight with you and sometimes it just walks away. Never let your bank account determine your value. Realize life ebbs and flows. When it shrinks back, readjust and move forward knowing it will flow again. Hold onto things loosely. Never let them hold you.

....

....

....

....

....

....

....

....

....

it's okay to stand alone

~ Don't be a joiner and trend follower. Find your most authentic you and work it! You don't need to join every bandwagon that rolls by. Have friends but don't change yourself, your values and character to stand with them.

....

....

....

....

....

....

....

....

....

....

NATALIE LAMB

honor yourself

∼ Sex is sacred, created by God for pleasure and to create life with your spouse. It was the gift He gave to create oneness. Society doesn't value this, but you should. Sex gives access to you, to your most vulnerable parts. Be wise. A quick rush of feelings and chemical highs can alter your life forever. Honor yourself above all else.

....

....

....

....

....

....

....

....

....

pause... and pause again

∽ When you feel your body desiring sex, pause, then pause again. And well, pause again! Be aware there is always a price to be paid. This power you hold can be easily given away but it will cost you emotionally, mentally, spiritually, as well as physically. Realize you can easily be depleted. The question is: "Will the results be worth what I will be giving away?"

. . . .

. . . .

. . . .

. . . .

. . . .

. . . .

. . . .

. . . .

count up the cost

～ Count the cost before any sexual activity begins. In the moment, awareness can be clouded or nonexistent. Remember, you can say no and change your mind at any time. Initial engagement doesn't guarantee completion. Anyone who doesn't honor this needs to be quickly dismissed from your life. Again, consider the cost first.

....

....

....

....

....

....

....

....

*lifetime love
requires friendship*

∼ Your partner should be your friend and companion. Look for someone you really like and can be with, even if it isn't fireworks. Don't get yourself caught up in fairy tales that don't exist. No one is saving you, no one is rescuing you. Your mate wants you to give and receive. They want to be held down as much as you want them to hold you up. They need a soft place as much as you need a soft place. Yes, the sexes are different in many ways but we have so many similarities. We are made of the same basic stuff and require the same basic things from each other. Find a partner that thinks this way and you will have a love for a lifetime. It really doesn't have to be that hard.

....

....

....

....

....

children are miracles from god

∽ Only have children when you are married, when you have a strong solid relationship, and after you both have had a lot of time to do you, whatever that is. Decide together that you are ready to add another love. Don't have a child out of a need to be loved, have a child out of the desire to *give* love. You are deciding to give life, to be a part of the miracle that God lets us partake in—do not take this lightly.

....

....

....

....

....

....

....

....

prepare for the challenge

~ Talk to your partner about how you view children and how you want to raise them. Get as close to the same page as possible. This will be the most important job you will ever do. Research, study, dissect, ask for advice but don't make it law, before you decide on your "how," and stay flexible. Pray for guidance. Ask God to prepare both of you for this challenge, for the life He is going to create to give you. Ask Him to show you the child's destiny. Ask Him to show you how to help them fulfill their destiny with the least number of scars. (You see, I didn't say *without* scars. Scars will happen. We are human. But scars don't have to be purposeful or extreme.) Then be prepared to mess up, fail, do it wrong, lose your temper (but never violently); ask for forgiveness, be open to letting your children teach you, be open to being wrong, etc. Look at it as a journey. In my opinion, this is one of the best journeys this life can offer.

....

....

freedom has a cost

∼ Live freely. But know freedom has a
cost. You must always be responsible with
your freedoms.

....

....

....

....

....

....

....

....

....

....

....

you will pay

∿ Sometimes it's easy to skimp on your obligations, but in the end, you will pay. You will pay by failing at the task. Or you may pay by having to put far more time into it. Or you may pay by people losing trust in you. But you will pay. Just take care of business as it arises. It'll save you so much time and aggravation and possibly your reputation.

....

....

....

....

....

....

....

....

forgive yourself

⁓ Forgive yourself for the bad choices you
make. Simply admit that it was the wrong
thing to do. Don't make excuses. Make
restitution if that is needed. Learn the lessons
from your poor choices and move forward
determined not to make those choices again.
Beating yourself up will only keep you stuck
and bound. No progress there.

....

....

....

....

....

....

....

....

no excuses... own it

～ Restrain from making excuses of any kind. The only power you have is your power of choice. We are forever choosing, so whatever you willingly participate in is yours to own. Learn to own it all so you can move forward. Keep in mind, if you become a person who is full of excuses and holds no personal responsibility, people will grow tired of you and you will appear dishonest and untrustworthy.

....

....

....

....

....

....

....

....

the power of the tongue

∼ Life and death are in the power of the tongue. Live with BUTS: "This is hard BUT I can do it ... My heart is broken BUT it will heal." We have the power to create, so create something positive. Your body's cells respond differently to positives and negatives. Be wise and speak positively.

....

....

....

....

....

....

....

....

it's a delicate balance

~ Know when to lean in and when to stand tall. It's a delicate balance. If you lean when you should stand firm, you could be destroyed. If you stand firm when you should lean in, you might be abandoned. It will be trial and error. You will mess up. Learn from it. Fail but keep trying. The issue is not in leaning in or standing firm, the issue is knowing when you need to do which one.

....

....

....

....

....

....

....

....

make you proud!

∼ Be able to honestly look at yourself in the mirror and be proud of who you are and what you have done. If your behaviors will prevent you from looking in the mirror with pride and appreciation, then stop them. In the morning before you leave your home, look at yourself and smile. The key is to have that same smile and feeling of pride at the end of each day!

....

....

....

....

....

....

....

....

I stand always as your cheerleader: *You can do it!* I know your strengths. I see your struggles. I love your essence. You are my heart and my breath, pure greatness in my eyes! I walk in front of you because I need to see what is coming your way. I walk beside you because we get to journey together, explore new things together. I walk behind you, so when you fall, I am there to catch you. I've got you surrounded, my love! And God has us both! We can't go wrong! When your vision gets dim, use my eyes to see yourself, and rise again to your greatness! I embrace your totality. I love you. Make YOU proud!

Notes

....

....

....

....

....

....

....

....

....

....

....

....

....

....

....

....

....

....

....

....

....

....

....

....

....

....

....

....

....

....

....

....

....

....

....

....

....

....

About the Author

Natalie Lamb is a life coach, educator, counselor, and speaker of over 20 years. She teaches how to choose purpose, freedom, and love, and her vision is to equip others with the power to change their lives. Natalie's coaching business, *It's Your Choice* offers classes, workshops and retreats on personal and spiritual development, as well as marriage counseling and parenting advice, providing informed ways to heal. She can be found at www.iyconline.com.

Works by Natalie Lamb

The Wisdom Chronicles

Open Your Eyes

What I Want You to Know

The Book of Wisdom

The Book of Ingenuity

The Book of Patience

The Book of Change

Inspirational Journal

My Wisdom Chronicle

·

Made in the USA
Columbia, SC
14 October 2024

43578857R00070